PHILIPPIANS:

LOVE LETTER FROM A SENIOR CITIZEN

PHILIPPIANS.

LOVE LETTER FROM
A SENIOR CITIZEN

ALGER FITCH

TABLE OF CONTENTS

Preface

Portland, Oregon's First Christian Church has named its older adult group "STARS." The acrostic stands for *Some Terrifically Active Retired Seniors*. What a significant title! But, Paul, the author of Philippians, doesn't totally fit the category. "Terrifically active" he is indeed. A "Senior" in years"? I would say so, with little hesitation. However, "Retired" is the term any reader of his busy schedule would have to question.

The brief thank-you note which is Philippians has tremendous insights to benefit Christians of every age from vigorous childhood to slower sunset years. It is the intention of this examination of inspired and inspiring text (Philippians) to highlight what God's servant Paul would have Seniors like himself to learn. How much stronger the church would be and how much more blessed the individual would become that listens with both ears wide open.

You are invited to walk with me down the well-marked road God wants His Saints (especially the Senior ones) to travel. It leads to inward joy and personal satisfaction. Keep your eyes peeled on our spiritual journey for the way-markers that point to joy "inexpressible and glorious" (I Peter 1:8), peace "which transcends all understanding" (Philippians 4:7), and love which "always protects, always trusts, always hopes, always perseveres" (I Corinthians 13:7).[1]

A young man may complain that after thirty years of service to one company all his father received at retirement to show for his faithful years was a gold watch. How different for God's servants after a life lived for Christ. The committed Christian knows that in the future there will be the "golden street"[2] but in the present there are "golden opportunities" beyond counting; plus "gold memories" of happy days gone by.

---

[1]All Scripture quotations unless otherwise noted will be from the *New International Version* (Grand Rapids: Zondervan, 1973).

[2]Revelation 21:21.

Introduction

The letter of Paul "to all the saints . . . in Philippi," like most every epistle from him comes in an envelope of "grace." That is, the opening lines will include that word "grace," as will the final sentence (cp. 1:2 and 4:23). Following the greeting, we hear the apostle break out in gratitude:

> I thank my God every time I remember you. In all my prayers for all of you, I always pray with joy because of your partnership in the gospel from the first day until now, being confident of this, that he who began a good work in you will carry it on to completion until the day of Christ Jesus (1:3-6).

That last thought of "completion until the day of Christ Jesus" makes clear to that congregation, our local fellowships or our personal lives that we are not yet finished products. We do not already have it made. No one of us has attained perfection. You may recall seeing the letters "G-I-N-F-W-M-Y" — *God Is Not Finished With Me Yet.*

When Jesus stated on the cross, "It is finished" (John 19:30), He meant His purpose in His first-coming was accomplished. The debt for sinners was paid in full. But His life was not over, for the crucifixion would be followed by the resurrection. His ministry was not ended, for He would continue interceding as our High Priest, serving as the "one mediator between God and men" (I Timothy 2:5).

At whatever age or state we have attained, it is important to keep in mind that we are not yet the final product. Our service to Jesus is not completed. And after all the letters the apostle had written, all the congregations he had founded and all the opponents he had silenced, he was not ready to cry out, "It is finished."

If the apostle was the "not-finished *author*" of the letter we study, and if the congregation addressed was a "not-finished *audience*," it should be crystal clear that we too need a wakeup call to our "not finished *assignment*."

We begin our hearing of the appeal, "We are not finished yet," asking three introductory questions: Why call the Epistle a "Love Letter?" Why call the Apostle a "Senior Citizen?" and Why call the application a "Needed Encouragement?"

Why Call the Epistle a "Love Letter?"

My students at Pacific Christian College of Hope

International University have heard me say that I do not limit my use of the term "Pastoral Epistles," as do most Bible teachers, to I and II Timothy and Titus. Every New Testament letter, by whatever various author, was written out of pastoral concern. Scholars began in the eighteenth century for the first time to use the phraseology Pastoral Epistles for only three of Paul's letters. Be it Paul or Peter, James or John, Jude or some other penman, each wrote because of genuine care for God's people.

Philippians can be termed a "thank you note." It may be labeled a "joy letter" or a "unity message." I also prefer naming it a "love letter." R.P. Martin called it "a window into Paul's personal and pastoral character."[1] Archibald M. Hunter evaluated it as "the most beautiful of Paul's letters."[2]

In its four chapters are 100 uses of the first person singular pronoun. As you read it afresh, look for "I," "me" and "my," as they keep appearing on each page. The usual beginning, "Paul an apostle of the Lord Jesus Christ" is absent. He is not penning a doctrinal thesis. Here he is conversing with personal friends who have meant so much to him "from the first day" (Philippians 1:5) when the gospel was planted in their city (cp. Acts 16).

This love letter overflows with mixed feelings. Joy is sensed on every page, but so are anxiety for their

---

[1]"Philippians," *New Century Bible* (Oliphant/Erdman, 1970), p. 12.

[2]*Philippians,* Laymen's Bible Commentary, Vol. 22 (Richmond: John Knox Press, 1959), p. 8.

condition and gratitude for their partnership. Love opens up a life for inexpressible moments of happiness, but also for hours of heartbreak. All these emotions radiate from each paragraph before us. This is a love letter indeed if you mean *agape*-love or intelligent good will.

Why Call the Apostle a "Senior Citizen?"

The Psalmist wrote that "the length of our days is seventy years — or eighty, if we have the strength" (Psalm 90:10). Fortunately, as we enter the 21st Century in the United States of America, that may be true with even better longevity in the future.

Such was seldom the case in Jesus' day and in the times following. On Christmas Day 1999 an article appeared in the Oregonian newspaper. It was written about Richard L. Rohrbaugh a New Testament scholar on the faculty of Portland's Lewis & Clark College. This professor, who chairs the social science section of the Society of Biblical Literature, claims that only 10% of the population in Jesus' day lived to age 45 with but 3% ever seeing 60. To quote him, "The average age of death for males was 27 years and for females 18."

While I do not instantly bow down to the views of liberal scholars, I am prone to accept what Scriptures say. Paul, a year or so before producing the Philippian letter, had written to Philemon, calling himself "Paul — an old man and now also a prisoner of Christ Jesus" (verse 9). Howard F. Vos in the conservative *Evangelical Commentary on the Bible* agrees: "Paul could indeed be considered an aged man because he was about sixty or older in a society where the normal life span was almost certainly under forty."[3] When Gerhard Kittel,[4] Gunther Bornkamm,[5] and Edward Lohse[6] add their "Amen," it would be foolhardy to disagree.

Luke had called Paul a "young man named Saul" (Acts 7:58) before his ministry began. He used the Greek word (νεανίας), which did not imply a teenager but someone between 24 and 40 according to Hippocrates. I assume that Paul was around 35 years old at his baptism, but now may be closer to his late fifties or early sixties. The chronology, for which some have hazarded a guess, would have the apostle to the Gentiles writing his earliest letters (Galatians, Thessalonians) at 49 or 50, his major doctrinal works at 55-56 (Romans, Corinthians) and the Prison Epistles

---

[3]Walter A. Elwell, ed. (Grand Rapids: Baker, 1989), p. 1121. In close agreement with this view see: Edgar J. Goodspeed, *Paul* (New York: Holt, Rinehart and Winston, 1947), p. 1; Michael Grant, *Saint Paul* (New York: Scribner, 1976), p. 12; J.L. Houlden, *Paul's Letters from Prison* (Philadelphia: The Westminster Press, 1970), p.16; Emil G. Kraeling, *I Have Kept the Faith* (Chicago: Rand McNally, 1965), p. 268; *New Catholic Encyclopedia* Volume 11 (New York: McGraw & Hill, 1967), p. 3; F.L. Cross, ed., *The Oxford Dictionary of the Christian Church* (London: Oxford University Press, 1974), p. 1046; Richard P. McBride, gen. ed., *The Harper Collins Encyclopedia of Catholicism* (San Francisco: Harper, 1995), p. 972.

[4]*Theological Dictionary of the New Testament,* Volume VI (Grand Rapids: Erdmans, 1964–76).

[5]*Paul* (New York: Harper & Row, 1971), p. XI.

[6]*Hermeneia: A Critical and Historical Commentary of the Bible: Colossians and Philemon,* Volume 12 (Philadelphia: Fortress Press, 1971).

(Colossians, Philemon, Ephesians, Philippians) at 61-62. This would leave I Timothy and Titus to be written perhaps at 64 years of age and II Timothy preceding his death at 67.

Allow for error a few years either direction in these educated guesses and Paul is still an "old man" with much to say to persons as they enter their golden years. What he wants all men or women to realize, as they ripen in their days, is that they are not finished in Christ's glad service. Their best years are yet ahead. "Gray hair is a crown of splendor" (Proverbs 16:31). Wear it well.

Why Call the Application a "Needed Encouragement?"

The encouraging words the aged apostle is about to give to Senior Saints show he has had his attitude on growing older shaped by his knowledge of Sacred Scripture. In the Psalms he had read that the righteous "planted in the house of the LORD . . . will flourish in the courts of our God. They will still bear fruit in old age, they will stay fresh and green" (92:12-14). He called to memory the words of Job that "with aged men is wisdom, and in length of days understanding" (12:12).

The believer's philosophy of life brings forth serenity and enables accepting and rising above adversity. People who focus on Jesus know that to stay youthful requires staying useful. Look around in the community where you live and find a man here and a lady there young at 80 or old at 25. Nobody grows old by merely living a certain number of years.

Bernard Baruch is reported as observing, "An older person can often do more in less time than his more physically spry junior. He has learned to pace himself. He knows the short-cuts — and the pitfalls. He has acquired judgment and stability."

Too many persons at 65 prematurely walk old, talk old and think old, as if retirement is a time to practice being dead. Paul holds the opposite view. He is convinced that aging is not something to be feared. It is not so much a time of life as a state of mind. Consider your years from this hour forward. Join the aging Paul to "shine like stars in the universe as you hold out the word of life" (Philippians 2:15-16).

If you consider for but one moment the importance of retirement years in our time, especially in the U.S.A., think what you can do for Christ's church. At this time in your life, with your many talents sharpened and your time more freed up, where does God need you in His church? Enter the ministry as never before. Darkness is in the world, and Christ's light is in the church.[7] Be a good steward and retire from your "tent-making" for a living, if you must, but never retire from using every talent, tithe and testimony in the work that lasts into eternity.

Some man in Illinois aged 106 gave counsel to all who would live to a ripe old age. The secret, he declared, is "Just keep from dying!" Don't you Christians die on the vine by no longer attending the assembly, singing in the choir, helping in the nursery,

---

[7] Cp. Matthew 5:14; John 8:12; Romans 13:11-14; Ephesians 5:8ff; Revelation 2:1, 5.

or working in the kitchen. The 104 verses of Philippians are Paul's personal, practical, and powerful words of encouragement for you to "give of your best to the Master." We will all need some financial resources to live on, but most of all we will need kingdom interests to live for. To be a radiant Saint, join Paul and Timothy in remaining "servants of Christ Jesus" (Philippians 1:1). Pray that the following chapters will sift out practical things from Paul's Philippian letter that will make more purposeful every further day or year Christ grants us. Keep in your mind that the book of the Bible we are studying is a love letter from a senior citizen and the needed encouragement to the reader is there for the asking.

I
SENIOR SAINTS NEVER FINISH SHOWING GOD'S LOVE

A rural man was being interviewed on his 102nd birthday. Since the old-timer was the oldest resident in the county, the newspaper editor asked to what he attributed his great age. The reply was, "It is very simple. I began taking vitamin tablets daily ever since I was 99."

Ever since he met Christ on the Damascus Road, Paul began taking in daily the love and grace of God. That is why from his conversion on, he is so different. From his mid-thirties at his baptism to his now early sixties, he is a changed man. This letter to the Philippian congregation, which itself is now approximately ten years old, reflects the One who "so loved the world that he gave his one and only Son, that whoever believes in him shall not perish but have eternal life" (John 3:16).

Philippians: Love Letter

In this epistle we will read: "It is right for me to feel this way about all of you, since I have you in my heart" (1:7). "I long for all of you with the affection of Christ Jesus" (1:8). "This is my prayer: that your love may abound more and more" (1:9). "If you have . . . any comfort from his love . . . then make my joy complete . . . having the same love" (2:1-2). Timothy, likewise, "takes a genuine interest in your welfare" (2:20). Epaphroditus, also, "longs for all of you" (2:26). Paul, himself, calls all the church members "my brothers, you whom I love and long for" (4:1).

To grasp the inclusiveness of the Apostle's affection, notice his frequent tie of the words "all" and "you" so no Saint would feel left out. Those in the United States known for saying "you all" in their speech are the Southerners — those below the Mason and Dixon line. That geographical location does not explain Paul. He is not in Arkansas, Alabama or Texas, but is beyond question "in Christ."

The pronoun "you" by itself is neither singular nor plural, but add the word "all" and the doubt is erased. When Paul writes to a single individual like Philemon, "Grace to you" (verse 3), the "you" refers to one man. When he pens his message to the Philippian church, "Grace to you" (1:2), the pronoun includes "all the saints in Christ Jesus at Philippi" (1:1). The letter is for more than some special friends or only the "overseers and deacons." In the earlier King James Version of the Bible "you all" appears in the first chapter of this New Testament book alone five times (verse 4, 8, 25, and two times in verse 7).

The "you all" (KJV) or "all of you" (NIV) in 2:17 and 4:21 clarify that to the author everyone matters. Not just one group or only certain individuals have meaning to God and His servants. All are important. One of the most attractive virtues of a local congregation is the personal self-esteem created by knowing every child of God is important to the Father and to all others in the family.

A. Senior Saints Never Finish Showing God's Love for the Churches, Wanting to Strengthen Them

Doesn't every church member hope and pray that his preacher feels with Paul, "I face daily the pressure of my concern for all the churches" (II Corinthians 12:28)? Or who does not wish for elders who can in all honesty ask, "Who is weak, and I do not feel weak? Who is led into sin, and I do not inwardly burn" (II Corinthians 12:29)?

"The fellowship of the concerned" would be a good description of a church living as Jesus designed it to live. Because you can make a difference in the local congregation to which you belong, immerse your mind daily in the cleansing power of love as Paul a few years before defined it in I Corinthians 13. What you exemplify will gradually be reflected in other lives around you. Put your personal name where the Apostle used the word "love." Say (your name) "is patient . . . kind . . . does not envy . . . does not boast . . . is not proud." Say of your church, "It is not rude . . . not self-seeking . . . not easily angered . . . keeps no record of wrongs." Say of your personal family, it "does not delight in evil but rejoices with truth . . . always protects . . . trusts . . . hopes . . . perseveres" (I Corinthians 13:4-7).

No one is more likely to affect a congregation's character to be more loving — more Christlike — more mature — than a senior citizen. White hair brings respect and shows the wisdom of years. That means as your years go on, you are ever more important to the local body of which you are a part — never less important. God needs you at this time of your life in the assembly. Your faithfulness shines. Your prayers matter. Your convictions, tested by time, become contagious. God is not finished with you yet. Tie in with Paul inviting those around you, "Join with others in following my example, brothers, and take note of those who live according to the pattern" (Philippians 3:17).

B. Senior Saints Never Finish Showing God's Love for the Lost, Wanting to Reach Them

In the perusal of the Pauline writings we meet a man who is convinced that if a faith is not satisfying, it ought to be given up; but if it is satisfying, it should be given away. He believed this the day he took Jesus into his life. He holds that still to be true, as he moves into what Hippocrates called the 6th of the 7 stages of human life. Although the preacher is in his 60s, he intends to remain both active and articulate in sharing the good news with others.

Can a lover quit talking about his beloved? Neither lip nor life can be silenced, no matter one's age, when the one you love fills your every thought. After Jerusalem arrest, Caesarea imprisonment, and now Roman confinement, Paul's interest is held by the "furtherance of the gospel" goal. That inner drive was there "from the first day until now" (1:5). Acts 16 introduces us to Lydia's household and that of a jailor. These were the earliest Europeans brought to salvation. Paul had received a call to introduce the gospel into Macedonia. Now these converts partner with the apostle to reach others, bringing them from darkness to light and from lostness to salvation.

"The progress of the gospel," (1:12, KJV) or the success of the mission, overcomes the barriers thrown against it. The gospel "has become clear throughout the whole palace guard and to everyone else" (1:13). Paul would like to see all of us "encouraged to speak the word of God more courageously and fearlessly" (1:14). "Caesar's household" (4:22) are potential believers, as certainly as Lydia's household or the jailor's household.

It is written of Lydia that "the members of her household were baptized" (Acts 16:15). That happy announcement can one day soon be written of your distant relatives and closer kin. It will only take your putting first things first and loving your extended family into God's family.

If there was ever a seemingly impossible consequence to follow Christian witnessing, it would be the record of a pagan jailor converting at the first hearing of the gospel. He had neither a previous knowledge of the Creator nor any awareness of the Old Covenant Scriptures. Yet, the Bible account reads that in the middle of night at the hearing of the message, "immediately he and all his family were baptized" (Acts 16:33).

Romans 10:17 reads that "Consequently faith comes from hearing the message." Check with your Bible today and you will find it still reads the same way. Give it a try. Love would motivate parents and grandparents especially to find time to speak to those closest to them. Without making it a priority it likely will not happen. With passion for the lost, personalized in those in your family or neighborhood, share your faith.

It is too good not to share. Love is the key to the hearts of humans. Get out your key. Express your love. You'll be glad you did. One thing for sure, there will be no soul winning in heaven. All who reach Paradise will have been won to Christ on earth. Paul did not know with absolute assurance that he would "go on living in the body," but while he would "remain in the body" (1:22, 24) there is no doubt to how he would use the days, months, or years. At whatever point death would come, he would be found "defending and confirming the gospel" (1:7). Let us be reminded that none of us are finished showing God's love to the lost. Keep on wanting to reach them.

C. Senior Saints Never Finish Showing God's Love for the Truth, Wanting to Defend It

As our generation enters the third millennium, loving the congregations and loving the lost is okay in our modern society. But loving the truth and wanting to defend it is to many not politically correct.

According to an article by David Gibson of Newark, New Jersey in the *Honolulu Star-Bulletin* of January 22, 2000[1] the headline reads: "The old invocation that there is 'one way' to salvation has been supplanted by new paths to spiritual fulfillment." He reports that the word "religion" has been replaced by the safer word "spirituality." What we have today is 2,500 distinct forms of Christianity served cafeteria style as megachurches model themselves as shopping malls competing for clients. Theology is played down and TV religionists offer a menu of options as the public seeks to find the spiritual concept that fits their lifestyle. Commitment is out. Repentance is old-fashioned. "To each his own" with "no norm required" is the acceptable ideal.

Paul will have none of that. He offers his best efforts for "defending and confirming the gospel" (1:7), claiming, "I am put here for the defense of the gospel" (1:16). He tells of his highest desire to "know (you Philippians) that you stand firm in one spirit contending as one man for the faith of the gospel without being frightened in any way by those who oppose you" (1:27-28). Let "every tongue confess that Jesus Christ is Lord" (2:11). Let every churchman and churchwoman "Watch out for those dogs, those men who do evil, those mutilators of the flesh" (3:2). Other persons may be "enemies of the cross of

---

[1]Section B, p. 1 ff.

Christ" (3:18). Let the Christians "stand firm in the Lord [as his] dear friends!" (4:1).

Christ brought God's truth to the world. In Paul's preaching in Macedonia the Philippians received the divinely given gospel. As other teachers come into the community altering that message, only the devil calls for total openness to all other ideas as acceptable options. One guru will swerve to the left and end up in lawlessness. Another dogmatic clergy-person will swerve to the right and end up in legalism. Paul will "contend for the faith that was once for all entrusted to the saints" (Jude 3). Only that gospel deserves to be protected and promoted. Libertine *self-indulgence* in the face of Christ's *self-sacrifice* is an enemy of the cross.

Even some church growth experts, should they advise lightening up on doctrine to avoid scaring away a "seeker," need to remember that Christ's parting order to teach "everything . . . commanded" (Matthew 28:20) includes His calls for repentance, commitment, and obedience.

The reason the writer of the letter we are studying was glad to be on trial before the Caesar of Rome was because his defense was a defense of Christ's gospel. That story he was ready to vindicate. "Speaking the truth in love" (Ephesians 4:15) is always in order. Attempting to be so politically correct that we neither find time nor place "for correcting and training in righteousness" (II Timothy 3:16) is the recipe for failure. Senior Saints, who love the church and love the lost, are needed to encourage the young to include love for God's revealed truth.

D. Senior Saints Never Finish Showing God's Love for the Savior, Wanting to Praise Him.

A *disciple* of Christ is one who *disciplines* his or her life by the teachings of the Master Teacher. Because of who that Teacher is and what He has done, "at the name of Jesus every knee should bow . . . and every tongue confess that Jesus Christ is Lord to the glory of God the Father" (2:10-11).

From the earliest days of Paul in the city of Philippi, the missionary is pictured as a worshiper "praying and singing hymns to God" (Acts 16:25). His hands were not raised in the direction of heaven but were fastened in the prison's stocks. His pew was not cushioned for comfort, but his body, severely flogged, could not discourage his heart from singing praise.

Now in another prison a decade later he begins his writing with, "I thank my God every time I remember you. In all my prayers for all of you, I always pray with joy" (1:3-4). His intercessory request is for his readers to be "filled with the fruit of righteousness that comes through Jesus Christ — to the glory and praise of God" (1:11). The followers of the Lord and Paul constitute the group who can say "we . . . worship by the Spirit of God . . . (and) glory in Christ Jesus" (3:3).

Bible scholars are confident that Philippians 2:6-11 is a hymn. For the many centuries of the church the hymns sung have reflected the convictions held by the worshiping church. No group is blessed more by the old hymns than the senior citizens who gather for worship each church assembly.

Philippians: Love Letter

When I had my 80th birthday, a small group of the town's businessmen over early morning coffee, listed for me the favorite hymns for people my age. There were ten of them. I remember but a few. One was "It Is Well with My Soul (but my back aches a lot)." Another was "Just a Slower Walk with Thee." Still another was "Go Tell It on the Mountain (but speak up so I can hear)." The one that made me laugh the most was "Guide Me, O Thou Great Jehovah (I've forgotten where I parked)."

Those hymns with their word changes may have brought a smile to my face, but all the worship-music of the past twenty centuries is always there for us to use showing love for the Savior as we praise Him. As the apostle had written about a year earlier than Philippians, "Speak to one another with psalms, hymns and spiritual songs. Sing and make music in your heart to the Lord" (Ephesians 5:19, cp. Colossians 3:16). Keep singing.

II

SENIOR SAINTS NEVER FINISH SMILING THROUGH ADVERSITY

Put on your sunglasses as we once again join Paul in that Roman jail cell. You might have expected it to be dark and gloomy, considering the trials that he has been under. But this man from Tarsus of Cilicia is a citizen of heaven's kingdom. He has early discovered that people on the way to heaven enjoy heaven on the way. It is no accident that Jesus taught that "the kingdom of heaven will be like" a wedding rather than a funeral (Matthew 25:1-10). Life in Christ is filled with sunshine and brimming with joyful promise. The weather report from glory is never partly cloudy with a 20% chance of rain. Those walking with Jesus, "the light of the world" (John 8:12), reflect His light in their faces.

The joy of which our Bibles speak is in no way related to the so-called "happy hour" at the corner tavern or the misnamed "holy laugh" or "Toronto blessing" that a small number of Pentecostals advocate. Frivolity is Satan's substitute for Christian joy. The joy about which the New Testament author writes is a settled state of mind characterized by inner peace in any of life's ups and down.

The Greek word (χαίρω) does not indicate some ecstatic rapture — some delirious exaltation. It rather describes a calm happiness or positive sense of wellbeing. Should one ask how any individual in Paul's shoes could be happy under such circumstances, the clear reply would be that followers of Jesus do not live under the circumstances into which life hurls them; they rise above those circumstances.

Let us walk through the chapters of our book of study where we will meet the word "joy" and its equivalents more often than in all his other letters combined. We notice that Paul, a living sample of what a Christian ought to be, does "always pray with joy" (1:4) and wherever "Christ is preached . . . [will] rejoice" (1:18). He seeks to find in his converts both "progress and joy in the faith" (1:25). Their unity is said to "make [his] joy complete" (2:2). Their service arising from their faith makes him "glad and rejoice" (2:17) and should cause them also to be "glad and rejoice" (2:18). We are not surprised at the plea regarding Epaphroditus that the congregation "welcome him in the Lord with great joy" (2:29) nor are we caught off guard that each one is admonished, "Finally, my brothers, rejoice in the Lord!" (3:1). Paul calls his "brothers . . . [his] joy and crown" (4:1) and gives the command, "Rejoice in the Lord always. I will say it again: Rejoice!" (4:4). He himself claims, "I rejoice greatly in the Lord!" (4:10).

The hymn of Chapter Two, regarding what Jesus has done, has created the frame of mind toward adversity that has produced the atmosphere of joy. This joy filters through all the thoughts expressed. No matter how tough life gets we are to "do everything without complaining or arguing" (2:14) — that is "without murmurings and questionings" (ASV).

To the inquiry "What must I do to be saved?" (Acts 16:30), Paul gave answer in the Book of Acts. If the present question becomes "What must I do to be happy?" the answer is in this Book of Philippians. The evangelist points to joy in supporting missions (1:5), in preaching Christ (1:18), in advancing unity (2:2), and it all begins by being in the Lord (3:1). He can sing with David, "Thou has put gladness in my heart" (Psalm 4:7). But we still cry out to know the secret of smiling in the face of adversity. We sit attentively before this book of joy ready to be taught the secret of this hero of yesterday who could affirm, "I have learned to be content whatever the circumstances. . . . I have learned the secret of being content in any and every situation" (4:11b-12). We ask our Rabbi or Professor Paul to bring his lesson on turning adversities into advantages, obstacles into opportunities and cramping difficulties into open doors.

A. Senior Saints Never Finish Smiling through the Adversity of Limiting Confinement

To teacher Paul, our first question is how hindrances can be viewed as helps, or blights be counted as blessings. We do want to get into heaven later, but we would desire to get some heaven into our lives now along the way. One would think that all the jail time and confinement[1] would have been enough to make any man *lose* his religion. It seems that to Paul it was enough to make him *use* his religion.

This letter admits its author knew "chains" (1:7, 13,14), "struggle" (1:30), "sacrifice" (2:17), "sufferings" (3:10, cp. 1:29), "need" (4:11,12), hunger (4:12) and "troubles" (4:14). Yet he also knew what the suffering of Christ on the cross had accomplished for good. When that crucified and risen Jesus called him through His spokesman Ananias, the reason given was open and clear: "This man is my chosen instrument to carry my name before the Gentiles and their kings and before the people of Israel. I will show him how much he must suffer for my name" (Acts 9:16). That call was being fulfilled. Paul was appearing for trial in Rome before the highest court in the Empire. He could say, "It has become clear throughout the whole palace guard and to everyone else that I am in chains for Christ" (1:14). He could

---

[1] In Philipppi (Acts 16:23); in Jerusalem (Acts 21:33 ff); in Caesarea (Acts 23:55); in Rome (Acts 28:16); elsewhere (II Corinthians 6:5; 11:23 ff).

pray, "I want to know Christ . . . and the fellowship of sharing in his sufferings" (3:10).

According to Jesus, following Him would inevitably demand denial and taking up one's cross (Matthew 16:24). It would be a false hope to believe that followers of the Messiah would never be "hungry . . . needing clothes . . . sick or in prison," when those situations are described as fitting their lot in this world (Matthew 25:37-39).

When you are bitterly disappointed, it helps to recall, your Savior was also. Hear Him lament over Jerusalem: "O Jerusalem, Jerusalem, . . . how often I have longed to gather your children together, as a hen gathers her chicks under her wings, but you were not willing" (Matthew 23:37). If you feel abandoned, hear Him cry out, "You do not want to leave too, do you?" (John 6:67). When you are filled with sorrow, bring to mind His words, "My soul is overwhelmed with sorrow to the point of death" (Matthew 26:38).

Can oil and water mix? Can joy and suffering ever blend together? Who can "rejoice in the Lord always" (Philippians 4:4) after being mobbed, beaten, stoned, cuffed and now facing life-threatening charges? The answer is: any believer in "the cross of Christ" (Philippians 3:18). The author of Hebrews writes that Jesus "for the joy set before him endured the cross" (12:2).

Paul could ask if *he* is the prisoner when chained to the wrist of a soldier. Or is it the other way around, and each soldier will be unable to escape as the soul-winner shares the gospel story one by one to the

Emperor's bodyguard. Every four-hour session with each guard has our zealous proclaimer claiming it "has really served to advance the gospel" (1:12). These guards soon came to know that this interesting man is not in a cell for some crime done, but for Christ. This unique case is a cause célèbre — something to tell about — and so the gospel spreads.

Should you ever find yourself "chained" to a wheelchair, or "chained" to a rest-home environment, or even "chained" to a job you don't really like, just call to mind, "The Lord is near" (4:5). You need not feel alone. You are "not to be anxious about anything." Worry solves nothing. Rather good results will come if "in everything by prayer and petition . . . [you] present your requests to God" (4:6). If you would find "the peace of God" (4:7), realize it comes only from the "God of peace" (4:9). Know that He knows. Rest assured He cares. Allow Him to lead.

We might consider Paul to be the cheerleader of the team who can turn a seeming defeat to a glorious victory. We can never *be totally* crushed by a seeming defeat, when we are *totally* dedicated to the man on the cross.

Pray that no difficulty makes you *bitter* since, with Jesus' help, it can make you *better*. "I have *learned* to be content whatever the circumstance," reads chapter 4:11. It takes a while to *learn* that secret, but it can be learned. Contentment, when things are difficult, does not come naturally, yet it can be learned by any who affirm "I can do everything through him who gives me strength" (4:13).

This promise is not to be taken out of context to mean I can walk on water, raise the dead, or fly to the moon and back in half a second. The previous verses speak of facing the circumstances that life throws your way and being content "whether well fed or hungry, whether living in plenty or in want" (4:12). Too many, I fear, can handle poverty better than they could handle wealth. Sensing a need for God in the person's life can be more threatened by striking oil on one's property than losing one's job.

May you find that the role of religion is not to furnish instant solutions to all life's perplexities. Its genuine place is to provide courage and help in facing those difficult situations. Paul's faith and yours may not lessen the number or intensity of dangers to be met along life's way, but it will provide the courage to meet those challenges with Christ at our side. A congregation is to be "contending as one man for the faith of the gospel without being frightened in any way" (1:28). A horse may shy away, hearing a rattlesnake on the path ahead. Christians, knowing that Jesus the conqueror of Satan the old serpent is with us, are emboldened and not intimidated. "You know," wrote James, "that the testing of your faith develops perseverance" (James 1:3). "All kinds of trials," added Peter, "come so that your faith . . . may be proved genuine and may result in praise, glory and honor when Jesus Christ is revealed" (I Peter 1:6-7). Paul's five years of continuous imprisonment never changed his mind. The apostle gave his face to God, and the Lord put the smile on it. He will do the same for your countenance. Just sing with the Psalmist,

"The precepts of the Lord are right, giving joy to the heart" (Psalm 19:8).

B. Senior Saints Never Finish Smiling through the Adversity of Failing Health

You may never in your senior years experience the confinement of a prison cell and show your faith, as did Paul and Silas, "about midnight . . . praying and singing hymns to God . . . [while] other prisoners were listening to them" (Acts 16:25). It may very well be failing health that is the hardship where your relationship with Jesus will shine forth and both encourage a grin and dispel grouch.

I read somewhere of a person facing the toughest time in his life. First, he got pyorrhea, followed by appendicitis. Just as he was recovering from these, he got pneumonia, followed by pulmonary phthisis and then eczema. Somehow he got over them just in time to get angina pectoris followed by arteriosclerosis. All in all he never knew how he pulled through. It was the hardest spelling test he had ever had.

Your actual physical sicknesses may prove to be a more critical test of faith for you. If such a time comes your way, does the biblical book of Philippians reveal any remedy to help you keep the smile in your heart?

The book points forward to the coming days of Christ's return when all of us will have bodies "like his glorious body." In the meantime the epistle makes us aware that before that transformation in the last day, we live in "our lowly bodies" (3:21). The ASV worded it, "the body of our humiliation." The ailing body can be humiliating to even Paul, who so often had to suffer. The KJV reads "vile body" which, in our century, gives a meaning of something utterly evil and horrible. In their sixteenth century English ("vile" from the Latin *vilis*), the translators were only conveying that the body, subject to decay and change, is of small worth compared to the glorious body that shall be ours in eternity.

Modern "divine-healers" may mislead some hurting souls to believe that every Christian has the "right" to a miraculous healing. Is that the case? Three individuals named in the Philippian letter can help us find God's answer to that question. They, as well, can provide us help in knowing what to do, should sickness come our way. Epaphroditus, Timothy and Paul are ready to bear witness on this question.

Chapter two speaks about Timothy in verses 19-24 and regarding Epaphroditus in 25-30. The congregation at Philippi had sent Epaphroditus to help Paul in prison caring for his needs. "You heard he was ill," Paul writes, adding, "Indeed he was ill, and almost died" (2:26-27). The action taken was to pray for their "brother, fellow worker and fellow soldier" (2:25). No instantaneous miracle of healing was demanded, but God's grace in this case was both asked for and received as "God had mercy on him, and not on him only but also on me," wrote the apostle, "to spare me sorrow upon sorrow" (2:27).

It is always right to lay our burdens before the Lord. We have all been given the privilege of prayer as we seek the will of the One who always knows best and does what is best. It is very questionable that in every case a miracle should be expected. Little children need to see parents and grandparents occasionally tackle big problems and lose, so they too can watch and learn how to handle loss. When in disappointments they see you praise God nevertheless, they are gaining knowledge on how to face real life with Christ always by their side.

Epaphroditus, grateful for returning health, becomes now the letter-bearer from Paul to the congregation at home. The experience through which he has come, supported by his Christian friends, has made him a better man. Do not grapes become wine only after they are crushed? Cannot suffering, even while not good in itself, work "for the good of those who love him, who have been called according to his purpose" (Romans 8:28)?

Regarding Timothy, Paul expresses gratitude, saying, "I have no one else like him, who takes a genuine interest in your welfare" (2:20). Perhaps knowing pain made him tender toward others in need, understanding what sickness and suffering was like. In a letter some two years later, Paul admonishes: "Stop drinking only water, and use a little wine because of your stomach and your frequent illnesses" (I Timothy 5:23). That loving advice doesn't sound like what Benny Hinn and other TV healers promise. They say "Expect a miracle — tonight can be your night."

We ask that if God used Paul as the channel to bring healing to others, why does he not simply lay hands on his beloved Timothy and call on God for instant healing? Isn't he, as an Apostle of Christ, in charge? Paul would be both the first to affirm and the last to deny God's power and love. But he knows the purpose of miracles and the place of intercessory prayer. Jesus, not Paul, is Lord. His will in every case must be sought and followed.

The apostle learned this when his own health faced adversity. He was given what he termed "a thorn in my flesh." He writes, "Three times I pleaded with the Lord to take it away from me" (II Corinthians 12:7-8). The hard-to-accept lesson was finally learned that not 100% of the time, when we ask for healing, is the answer "yes and right now." This senior saint, the apostle Paul, has passed the test of smiling through adversity. As the old Bulgarian Proverb goes, "God promises a safe landing, but not a calm passage." The fragrance of homemade bread can only be created by baking in the hot oven.

C. Senior Saints Never Finish Smiling through the Adversity of Approaching Death

Here and there a human may get through many years of life without having the personal experience of either limiting confinement or failing health. Yet, since the time of Adam, close to 100% have had to face the reality of approaching death. In this life we dwell in "mortal bodies" (Romans 8:11), or "lowly bodies" (Philippians 3:21). Can these present bodies, ever subject to weakness, temptation, disease, and death, still wear a smile?

Let me call your attention to the two shortest verses in the Bible. One is "Be joyful always" in I Thessalonians 5:16. The other is "Jesus wept" in John 11:35. Jesus' tears were not because Lazarus had died. He knew what awaited this brother of Mary and Martha on the other side. His heart was broken that Lazarus' sisters thought for a moment that His delay to come immediately at their bidding meant He did not care. The short verse that "Jesus wept" carries the eternal truth that He always cares. Even when you and I "walk through the valley of the shadow of death," there will be nothing to fear for He will be with us (Psalm 23:4).

Paul, awaiting the outcome of his trial, is optimistic, writing, "I will continue to rejoice, for I know that through your prayers and the help given by the Spirit of Jesus Christ, what has happened to me will turn out for my deliverance. I eagerly expect and hope . . . Christ will be exalted in my body, whether by life or by death" (1:18-20). To the believer both life and death have meaning.

He continues, "to me, to live is Christ and to die is gain" (1:21). Understand that dying is only gain to one who precedes such demise by living "in Christ." When Paul will eventually die, by being beheaded outside Rome as a martyr, he will yet be staring death in the face unperturbed. Our generation hides the reality of death. We would rather protect our children from seeing it, not taking them to a funeral. We would prefer, by any means in the hospital, to postpone by medical powers the inevitable close of a life already beyond the point of no return. Hiding death, because of dread, the funeral parlor with cosmetic touches covers death's reality.

Paul rather sees two options open to him and other Christians like him. Either option is attractive.

To one of God's saints death is not looked at as an escape from hardship but an entrance to joy. The concept of death held by Christ's spokesman is neither a passing through purgatorial fires nor an entering a soul sleep of unconsciousness. Those consequences could never be ranked as "gain" (1:21). What would be gain indeed would be "to depart and be with Christ, which is better by far" (1:23). To "depart," (to break anchor, if you think as a boatsman, or to strike tent, if you think as a soldier) was a metaphor for death.[2]

God had granted Paul a foretaste of the next world, when he "was caught up to paradise . . . [hearing] inexpressible things" (II Corinthians 12:4). He can only agree with Isaiah (in 64:4) when he declared "No eye has seen, no ear has heard, no mind has conceived what God has prepared for those who love him" (I Corinthians 2:9). This much he can avow to the Philippians, "to depart and be with Christ, . . . is better by far" (1:23). Heaven is better — far better — very far better than any place on earth. Join Paul in wanting to take as many along with you as possible.

As Jesus promised the dying thief, who had asked from the cross to be remembered in Christ's kingdom, "I tell you the truth, today you will be with me in paradise" (Luke 23:43). So Paul assured the Corinthians, "We are confident . . . and would prefer to be away from the body and at home with the Lord" (II Corinthians 5:8).

---

[2] II Timothy 4:6; II Corinthians 5:1.

With all the urge to go, there is as option number two the desire to stay. Being with Christ or being with the church at Philippi are both high hopes. Death will culminate in going to the Lord, while release will result in returning to the Philippians. Desire yields to duty when the conclusion is reached, "It is more necessary for you that I remain in the body. Convinced of this, I know that I will remain, and will continue with all of you for your progress and joy in the faith" (1:24-25).

Bodily resurrections will take place at the day of Christ's return.[3] The human spirit leaving to dwell with Jesus continues to occur on the day one of God's saints is called home. Those with "names (that) are in the book of life" (4:3) have hope. "Our citizenship is in heaven" (3:20), so death is going home.

It is argued that putting a fence around a cemetery is totally unnecessary, for those inside cannot get out and no one outside wants to get in. Paul builds no wall against either option. God's man or lady can smile at whatever choice Christ makes for us. The sting of death is removed for those who trust in the resurrected Lord.

D. Senior Saints Never Finish Smiling through the Adversity of Opposing Doctrine

To be ill is not a good feeling. To be incarcerated and no longer free to minister as you planned is hard to take. To know that your death may come sooner

---

[3] 3:11.

rather than later may bring qualms in your emotions. But to have strong opposition tearing down the teaching for which you have given your all and disrupting the congregations you have established is the bitterest pill of all to swallow.

In this love letter, so filled with joy, it appears almost surprising to hear the warning shout, "Watch out for those dogs, those men who do evil, those mutilators of the flesh" (3:2). The ASV translates "Beware . . . beware . . . beware." What causes Paul, close to halfway[4] through his epistle, to write "Finally, my brothers," yet continue with so much more to say? The word "finally" might better be translated "furthermore" or "in addition."

The third chapter of the Philippian letter finds Paul explaining, "It is no trouble for me to write the same things to you again, and it is a safeguard for you" (3:1). The "same things" refer to ideas found earlier in this letter. In the first chapter he had spoken of his concern for "defending and confirming the gospel" (1:7) giving "knowledge and depth of insight" (1:9). There he also reminds his readers that, while some "preach Christ out of envy and rivalry" he is put here for the defense of the gospel" (1:15-16). His opponents "preach Christ out of selfish ambition, not sincerity, supposing that they can stir up trouble" (1:18). The believing church is to "stand firm in one spirit, contending as one man for the faith of the gospel without being frightened in any way by those who oppose" (1:27-28).

---

[4] 40% of the letter is yet to come.

A shepherd entrusted with a group of sheep is not faithful in his responsibility unless he uses "rod and staff" to hold off ravenous wolves set on destroying and scattering God's flock.[5] Paul knows what harm came to the newly founded churches of Galatia when Judaizers came from Jerusalem. They had not come to Antioch, Iconium, Lystra, or Derbe to establish a new work, they had come into Christian communities already established. These men had the one intention to steal sheep out of another's fold. The Galatian letter was written to meet this dangerous error, as were the letters sent from the Jerusalem conference called to squelch early this false teaching coming from self-appointed emissaries (Acts 15:23-29).

Such upsetting teaching had not yet come into the Macedonian area. Yet, while it was not a present danger, it was a potential threat. Doctors tell us that cancer discovered early may be successfully treated. The danger is to ignore the early signs until it is too late to stop the disease. Paul knows the peril of tolerating a threat to the gospel, by allowing a fatal doctrine to establish itself until it can not be successfully uprooted.

If "dogs" sounds too harsh a term to use in our "open-to-everything" day, remember how the God-inspired prophet John the Baptist called some religionists a "brood of vipers!" (Matthew 3:7), and God's only begotten Son named false prophets "ferocious wolves" (Matthew 7:15). "Dogs" was the ter-

---

[5]Acts 20:28-29, cp. Ezekiel 33:2-6.

minology the Jews had used to describe Gentiles. Paul takes their word and turns it back on them. If scavenger dogs roam about, barking and biting, that description fits the character of teachers set upon attacking the Christian gospel. Their growling at Paul and snapping at his heels is not constructive to the truth, but rather destructive and a threat to winning the world.

"Men who do evil" rightly defines the conduct of the fanatic errorists out to seduce Paul's converts, replacing the freedom Christ brings with the binding chains of legalism. "Mutilators of the flesh" correctly depicts those who insist that every Gentile become circumcised or be lost eternally. Making a play on Greek words, similar in sound but opposite in meaning, the Apostle uses the Greek words *katatome* and *peritome* (κατατομή and περιτομή). The first word means mutilation; the second is circumcision. To Paul the circumcision that saves[6] is one the Heavenly Father performs upon the human heart to remove all the evil there. The knife-men, or Judaizers, that seek to use the knife on Gentiles and cut away the flesh, are making shambles of the genuine gospel.

The true gospel that saves is the work of God through the cross. The false gospel that deceives puts pride in man's attainments. To counter such ego-centric haughtiness, Paul lists what he could have claimed if salvation could come by self-achievement. Such a list of good works on his part he classifies as "rubbish" (3:8). Can any Judaizer list more "browny-

---

[6]Romans 2:28-29; Colossians 2:11-12.

43

points" than Paul? Some claims have to do with heritage or the advantages by birth (3:7-9). Others are based on choice or self-achievement. He was an Israelite by birth, a Benjaminite by tribe, and Hebrew by blood. He lived by the law in Phariseean tradition. He showed national zeal in persecuting the church. He met rightous standards and was faultless in public eyes.

Natural birth plus personal zeal and work can never attain perfection. Only by Christ's work is salvation possible. The apostle's *dissatisfaction* with the false-teachers is their *self-satisfaction*. Their false perfectionism is a far cry from the more humble Christian view that perfection is the goal toward which we strive,[7] while knowing that its full attainment is in the future.

Paul, the forgiven man in Christ, is "confident of this, that he who began a good work . . . will carry it on to completion until the day of Christ Jesus" (1:6). He writes, after being Christ's follower for a quarter of a century, "Not that I have already obtained all this, or have already been made perfect, but I press on to take hold of that for which Christ Jesus took hold of me" (3:12-14). Read the rest of the chapter and ask, "Have I arrived? Is there nothing more for me to achieve?" The needed reminder "the prize for which God has called [us] heavenward" (3:14) is granted in the future. For while now "our citizenship is in heaven and we eagerly await a Savior from there" (3:20), as long as we are in "our lowly bodies" and

---

[7]Matthew 5:48.

not yet at the goal of our ultimate "glorious body," (3:21) we have a ways to go.

It is easier to see how the present title we wear, "saints in Christ Jesus" (1:1), does not imply we have attained perfection yet than it is to understand how we can "rejoice in the Lord" (3:1) while we face so many opponents.

Paul answers that, although his opponents supposed they could stir up trouble for him while he was in chains, "what does it matter? The important thing is that in every way, whether from false motives or true, Christ is preached. And because of this I rejoice" (1:17-18). The slandered Apostle is still optimistic that every effort to discredit the gospel would nevertheless lead to its investigation and the potential conversion of the honest explorers.

There is one wrinkle on this Senior Saint's face that no cosmetician's formula for wrinkle removal sold at Philippi's drug store can delete. That wrinkle on Paul's face is called a smile. It is visible on the countenance of all who "stand firm in the Lord" (4:1).

III

SENIOR SAINTS NEVER FINISH SUPPORTING THE MISSION

If one's personal aim is "to advance the gospel" (1:12), a congregation's "partnership in the gospel" (1:5) is the necessary ingredient to insure success. Paul's witnessing, plus Philippian backing "from the first day until now," added up to a winning combination. My hat is off to all faithful stewards who, over their working years, have supported the church in its mission, and now are retired from their employment in the secular world but have never retired from supporting the mission Christ gave His church.

Senior Saints are not to be found in the grandstands of some congregation, but on the playing field more than ever before. Poverty is not in having little but rather in doing very little worthwhile. To look forward to retirement years, when there will be nothing one has to do, is to misunderstand where real satisfaction can be found. Finding purpose and meaning in Christian work, as a partner with Jesus in reaching the world, is to have discovered the secret of abiding happiness.

Work at the highest calling is more fulfilling than play. Church work is only drudgery to a person with the wrong frame of mind toward it. The four-letter word "work" describes the best way man has ever invented to escape boredom. Was it not George Bernard Shaw who defined hell as "an endless vacation?" A youth is reported to have asked a lonely retiree what he felt was "life's heaviest burden." The terse, but long-pondered reply, was "to have nothing to carry."

Do not tell me what you would do if you had a better education or if you possessed a million dollars. What matters is what you do with the talents, time, and tithes that are now at your disposal. A follower of Jesus should not at any age be seeking some "lounge," where precious hours can be frittered away or valuable monies can be used up. To spend every resource to purchase items that will help relax your body or mind only temporarily will be to find those means are now buried for good and gone forever.

"Progress of the gospel" (1:12, ASV) ought to be our motivating drive. Paul, the Senior Saint writing to the church at Philippi, finds satisfaction in realizing that now, after his investment in the Roman imprisonment along with the Philippians' partnership, has produced a praetorian guard that has heard of Jesus (1:13) and brethren that have been inspired to boldly testify (1:14).

I am sure you would like to leave footprints in the sands of time. To do so you will need to still wear working shoes in your retirement years. Henry Van Dyke reminds us of the biblical truth that:

> This is the gospel of labor —
> Ring it, ye bells of the kirk —
> The Lord of love came down from above
> To live with the men who work.
> This is the rose he planted
> Here in the thorn-cursed soil:
> Heaven is blessed with perfect rest
> But the blessing of earth is toil.

A. Senior Saints Never Finish Supporting the Mission with Financial Boosts

A "fellow soldier" (2:25) in Christ's army should expect to hear the command "*Ready! Aim! Fire!*" Paul is "*ready* to preach the gospel . . . in Rome" (Romans 1:15). His single *aim* is "the defense of the gospel" (Philippians 1:16). He is on *fire* to fulfill that mission, writing, "One thing I do . . . straining toward what is ahead" (3:13). With him, as fellow-laborers, stand the members of the Philippian congregation enjoying "partnership in the gospel" (1:5).

"Partnership" or "fellowship" (ASV) are English words used to express the meaning of Paul's Greek term *koinonia* (κοινωνία).[1] While the accent in the Greek language properly falls at the end of the word,

---

[1] Philippians 1:4-11, 24-30; 2:1-4, 17-30; 3:10-11, 17; 4:1-3,10,14-18.

shifting it to the first syllable may keep us from missing a part of the meaning. Say aloud KOIN and the "coin of the realm" comes to mind, as a part of the message in the term. The modern "fellowship" word in old English was fee-lay-ship. When one person contributes a fee and others join in laying their fees into a common receptacle, each has had "fee-lay-ship" or fellowship in sharing to meet a felt need in the community.

Later, in this thank you note to the church for the gifts brought by Epaphroditus to the imprisoned Apostle, Paul writes, "No church had fellowship with me in the matter of giving and receiving but ye only" (4:15, ASV). In the verse "fellowship" beyond doubt includes financial sharing. Their generosity likely rented lodging in Rome for Paul. He knew and wrote: Epaphroditus was "sent to take care of my needs" (2:25).

When you partner with a missionary to help that fellow worker accomplish his or her task, financial boosts join with your prayers and correspondence to lighten the heavy load being carried. No ministry is more needed on the mission field than to know of a "loyal yokefellow" (4:3) at the home base.

Am I geting too personal — that is too "purse-and-all?" You may be thinking how small your pension is. The Macedonian churches, of which Philippi is one, were poor in wealth but rich in liberality. Their example is held up before others as commendable. It is written, "We want you to know about the grace that God has given the Macedonian churches." He explains, "Out of the most severe trial, their overflowing joy and their extreme poverty welled up in rich generosity. For I testify that they gave as much as they were able, and even beyond their ability." The most commendable fact, writes Paul, is that this was "entirely on their own" (II Corinthians 8:1-3).

All Christian giving is voluntary. The Philippians' giving to God's work was not only free-will in nature but consistent over the years. When the congregation was but a few months old, they gave assistance to the new work in Thessalonica. God's emissary, who started their church, compliments their long-standing generosity. He pens, "In the early days of your acquaintance with this gospel . . . even when I was in Thessalonica, you sent me aid again and again when I was in need" (4:16).

That kind of partnership in helping spread the gospel in new and distant places is the need of the hour. The 21st-century missionary could respond today as this apostle to the Gentiles wrote long ago, "The gifts you sent . . . are a fragrant offering, an acceptable sacrifice, pleasing to God. And my God will meet all your needs according to his glorious riches in Christ Jesus" (4:18-19).

The usual epistle greeting beginning any of Paul's letters has added to it in this instance the additional phrase "with the overseers and deacons" (1:1). A possible reason for this may be that the intention of the letter is to express gratitude for gifts brought to Paul. Such a transfer of funds would have come with the blessing and awareness of the congregational leaders. Well versed in their Bible (the Old Testament) they would know the time-proven adages that "A generous man will prosper; [while] he who refreshes others will himself be refreshed" (Proverbs 11:25) and that "He who is kind to the poor lends to the Lord, and he will reward him for what he has done" (Proverbs 19:17).

It is written in history books that Alexander the Great's father, Philip II of Macedon, outfitted his army from the rich gold and silver mines that once were in the vicinity of Philippi. Those mines have long been depleted. However the rich mines of Scripture truth in Paul's Philippian letter will never be exhausted. The spiritual gold to equip God's army in every generation is available to any Bible reader who will dig into the text. Digging into the mother-lode of the Philippian letter from a Senior Saint perspective, it shines forth with the treasured insight that whatever our age in years we are never finished supporting the mission with financial boosts.

B. Senior Saints Never Finish Supporting the Mission with Encouraging Words

There are missionaries who have remained on difficult mission fields because someone gave a word of encouragement at a very trying time. There are young ministers who have contemplated resigning from their first church when criticisms seemed prevalent and supportive "amens" were nowhere to be heard. It may only take a kind smile or uplifting comment from a Senior Saint to set the young preacher back to the work to which Christ called him.

Shepherding a flock is an awesome responsibility

and often a difficult task. With eyes alert to the wolves threatening from the outside and when all one's ears hear are bleatings from the sheep, ever saying "baa baa," the voice of appreciation from but one fellow shepherd may make all the difference in the world.

You may only have a widow's "mite" (Luke 21:2) to support the mission with a financial boost, but you have the priceless opportunity to give out generously appreciative words to God's servants. Those who help in the nursery, work with the youth, or sing in the choir appreciate the uplift of the words, "Well done, good and faithful servant!" (Matthew 25:21).

The Philippian letter is overflowing with titles that build self-esteem. The members are called "saints" (1:1), "dear friends" (1:12; 4:1), and "brothers . . . whom I love" (4:1). Their service to Christ is commended on every page and they find themselves said to be the reason for Paul's joy and gratitude to God (1:3-4).

I can just see now what a difference you can make in getting other workers into the field of labor and giving these servants in Christ's cause the staying power to remain on the job. You may say, "But, just because encouraging words from the well-known Apostle have such results, I am an unknown believer of few talents."

Let me remind you that most of the church's victories have been won over the centuries by obscure people. When you read in this Philippian letter of names like Euodia, Syntyche, or Clement or of the long list of names in Romans 16, there is no information of who these people were. Just a month ago I was in Southern California to encourage ethnic ministers. A former Cambodian student of mine from Pacific Christian College told me of the Church's growth in Cambodia. In the last ten years the number of believers in Christ has grown from 200 to an esimated 60,000. No "big name" stands out. It was done by very common people — laymen, if you please — letting God use them.

Singing was never intended to be limited to those with voices like that of Caruso, nor painting pictures to artists of the stature of Raphael. Telling of Jesus or encouraging others with letters was never meant to be the exclusive ministry of orators like Apollos or penmen like Paul.

No letter you write will appear in the next version of the New Testament. Yet there is a vital place in God's plan for short notes like the ones the aged John wrote to a "lady and her children" (II John 1) or to the "dear friend Gaius" (III John 1). Your oral words in person or over the phone will do much good. But also, so will your written words by mail through the post office or e-mail over your computer. Ministry by mail may be where you fit into the plan. Paul's letter was the next best substitute for his personal presence at Philippi. Say with him, "It is no trouble for me to write . . . to you again." (3:1).

As the author of Philippians puts pen to paper to write this letter at about 62 years of age, he could say, "I'm not finished yet," even regarding letter writing. His Pastoral Letters, with all their encouraging words, will be written between two to five years later. I'm grateful that Paul took time to write Philippians and the other prison epistles which have proved such a blessing to our world. Believe me, to someone out there in ministry, your short letters will certainly benefit others for Christ.

C. Senior Saints Never Finish Supporting the Mission with Personal Visits

Paul, who sends prayers to heaven and letters to congregations, wisely also sends to Philippi representatives (such as Ephaphroditus now[2] and Timothy later[3]). At the original founding of the congregation, the apostle had left Luke in the city for its first six years. The distance Epaphroditus and Timothy will be covering will call for a journey of five to seven weeks. The distance is about 800 miles. Once their boat docks on the shores of the Aegean Sea, there will still be ten more land miles to reach the city.

Epaphroditus is called the church's "messenger." That is, literally, the congregations' apostle (ἀπόστολος). He was not an apostle of Christ, being personally chosen and empowered as an official witness to the resurrection of Jesus. His office was apostle, or missionary, of the local church that sent him with an assigned task (cp. II Corinthians 8:23).

You see what these facts have to say to a congregation today. My congregation, like yours, can send money to help the cause elsewhere. They can write or communicate encouraging messages. They can send short-term workers, as Philippi commissioned Epaph-

---

[2]2:25-30.
[3]2:19-23.

roditus to meet needs on the distant field. Upon retirement from eight-hour days and five-day weeks, your pen and ink can serve well, but so can your specialized talents coupled with some free time.

If you want to be useful in fulfilling Jesus' great commission, ask a missionary suppported by your group if your abilities could be of help for a limited time in the country being served. Only be sure to go not as a tourist, but as a "fellow worker and fellow soldier" (2:25) for that stay. Be sure you avoid using up any mission funds or missionary's time. Rather lift the load from his or her shoulders.

Any earthly friendships made will continue into eternity. Once you have left home to be a blessing, you will come home burning to go back again and volunteering to do more at home than you ever did before. Why sit at home only counting time, when you can go on a mission and make time count. Regarding the early church it is stated "they went everywhere preaching the word" (Acts 8:4, ASV). Don't allow future biographers to write of you that you, in retirement, simply "went everywhere," but left out helping Christ's cause to others.

D. Senior Saints Never Finish Supporting the Mission with Intercessory Prayers

Most every letter from Paul, after the greeting "Grace and peace to you from God our Father and the Lord Jesus Christ" (1:2), breaks into prayer. This he does in our letter of study (1:3-4,9-11). He is also quick to attribute his awaited release from prison to their prayers for him. Listen to him name the cause for the anticipated result: "I know that through your prayers and the help given by the Spirit of Jesus Christ, what has happened to me will turn out for my deliverance" (1:19). Toward the end of the note he will restate the lesson learned from a life of prayer: "In everything by prayer and petition, with thanksgiving, present your requests to God" (4:6).

The request "Lord, teach us to pray" (Luke 11:1) could well become the Senior Saint's first petition after reaching the ages of 55 or 65. To help the church in its mission, let every spare moment become a prayer moment. Check even today if the rug before your mirror shows more wear than the one before your bed.

There may be little more you can do for the Christian workers on a foreign field than to lift their arms lest they fall down. Bible writers never fail to urge God's people to pray and to pray fervently as did Elijah (James 5:17). Only prayers that flow from the depth of our hearts have promise of reaching to heaven. Consider prayer the intercontinental ballistic missile for Christians to make the missionary cause advance in a new land. Prayer, by you, can be directed from your room to any point on the globe. That prayer-missile will leave your heart with great force and land at its destination with divine accuracy. Since God provided His workers with such a powerful weapon, it would be sad if it was seldom used in the battle for souls.

A car without a motor will not carry you very far. A church without prayer will never reach the destination to which our Master calls us.

IV

SENIOR SAINTS NEVER FINISH UNIFYING THE WORKERS

This Epistle of love, of joy, and of gospel advancement clearly deserves those descriptions because the terms "love," "joy" and "partnership in the gospel" keep radiating off the manuscript. A congregation is blessed when its Senior Saints model for all the rest the rich meaning of these qualities of maturity. As the Senior Paul could invite that congregation, "Join with others in following my example, brothers" (3:17), you can let your life model what dependability and faithfulness are to your church community.

A fourth key word to unlock this short New Testament lettter is "unity" or "harmony." "Love" demands it. There will be no "joy" without it. Where oneness is lost, "furtherance of the gospel" (1:5, ASV) ends. Paul pleads, "Conduct yourselves in a manner worthy of the gospel of Christ" that demands "You stand firm in one spirit, contending as one man for the faith of the gospel" (1:27). Such a plea for unity in Chapter One is followed by four incentives to harmony. Here is the call for the attitudes and actions required if oneness is to exist in any flock of God's sheep. Listen to the heart-cry of God's spokesman to this people so dear to him.

> If you have any encouragement from being united with Christ, if any comfort from his love, if any fellowship with the Spirit, if any tenderness and compassion, then make my joy complete by being like-minded, having the same love, being one in spirit and purpose (2:1-2).

This congregation had from the beginning reflected wonderful unity in Christ. The earliest members included the wealthy (such as Lydia, from the top bracket of society), the penniless (such as the slave girl ventriloquist who made a fortune for her master but none for herself), and the salaried (such as the Jailor, a Roman officer of middle class). But now more recently two women, who earlier "*contended* at (Paul's) side in the cause of the gospel" (4:3), are presently in *contention*. Partners formerly are becoming opponents presently. Those once *content* are now *contentious*. They are not living up to their personal names, for Euodia means "*prosperous* journey" and Syntyche means "*pleasant* acquaintance." When God's servants become *unpleasant*, no work by them will *prosper*.

In any situation like this, bringing harmony takes priority. Outsiders harassing the evangelist is bad enough, but insiders dividing from one another is even more fatal to the expansion of Christianity. Hence the priority plea to a coworker is, "Yes, and I ask you, loyal yokefellow, help these women who have contended at my side in the cause of the gospel" (4:3).

There can be no room for dissension in a church (or, between churches), if gospel work is to advance unhindered. Let some of "the overseers and deacons" (1:1) act quickly. Let one of Lydia's workers or the Jailor's family intercede posthaste. Or, better yet, let all the members together step in. In no case allow disharmony to continue on to the detriment and demise of the redemption story.

Churches in the Restoration Movement of the last century have set Christian Unity as their polar star. With all the victories won over the many decades in calling for the return to New Testament faith and practice, denominational division and sectarian pride are still with us. Can this book of Philippians help us identify the barriers that divide? Can this "love letter" guide us to be more successful tomorrow in bringing answer to our Savior's prayer that all who believe in Him "be one" (John 17:20-21)?

A. Senior Saints Never Finish Unifying the Workers by Being More Consistent in Prayer

One truth may have been so close to us we might not have seen it. As a parent may have said to you as a child, "If it were a snake, it could have bitten you." We have preached about Christian Unity. We have read books and magazine articles on the subject. We have been in conferences and conventions where the unity of believers was the central theme. As good and important as all of these were and are and ever will be, pay prime attention to what Jesus did. He prayed for unity. That is the burden of Christ's high-priestly prayer on the way to the cross. He had with clear insight taught, "Every kingdom divided against itself will be ruined, and every city or household divided against itself will not stand" (Matthew 12:25). The danger was too great that this Devil-inspired division could threaten God's kingdom — God's household. This situation called for the greatest power to be marshalled against it and that undefeatable power is prayer. We who have so long "stood" for unity, need to be ready to "kneel" and attain it. Paul saw prayer as the cure for many dilemmas that face the believers. He asked churches to join him and pray for his safety,[1] for his courage to prevail,[2] for his teaching to be clear,[3] and for his work to continue.[4] Having referred to the division rearing its head in Philippi around Euodia and Syntyche (4:1-3), he now calls out that "in everything . . . [through] prayer and petition" they should find "the peace of God, which transcends all understanding" (4:6). If He who hears our prayers is "the God of peace" (4:9), then the *giver* is the Lord and the *gift* is His peace. Prayer is the condition of peace — the cure for the present disorder.

---

[1]Romans 15:30-31; II Corinthians 1:10-11; II Thessalonians 3:2; Philemon 22.

[2]Ephesians 6:19.

[3]Colossians 4:3-4.

[4]II Thessalonians 3:1.

Paul's confidence is that his release, the church's victory, and the present problem's solution will be based on mutual prayer. He will pray for them and he knows they will be praying for him.

Prayerful people will be peaceful people. Let there be, on our part, more prayer and less pride, more cheering and less chiding, more priorities and less trivia in our search for congregational oneness.

B. Senior Saints Never Finish Unifying the Workers by Being More Humble in Attitude

There will never be unity without prayer, for prayer changes things. And more importantly prayer changes people, especially those persons who pray. Those who properly address their plea to "God our Father and the Lord Jesus Christ" (1:2), see themselves in the correct perspective as but "servants," as did "Paul and Timothy" (1:1). Only the *lowly minded* are apt to become "*like minded*" (2:2). That is to say, that an humble attitude is the key to unity. Oneness in the family of God requires that we "do nothing out of selfish ambition or vain conceit, but in humility consider others better than (ourselves)" (2:3). They who really want the unity for which Jesus prayed are required to "each . . . look not only to (our) own interests, but also to the interests of others" (2:4).

Harmony grows out of the soil of humility. Proper relationships cannot thrive where there are not proper attitudes. Our teacher Paul is ready to give the hardest lesson for many disciples to grasp. The way to unity is the one-lane road to humility. There is no other way to get to this destination of harmony. Self-centeredness only leads to division. The way of Christ (2:5-8) followed by Timothy (2:19-24), Epaphroditus (2:25-30) and Paul (3:4-21) is the only way to unity in Christ's body the church.

The inspiring hymn of 2:5-11 is not used by Paul as testimony to his firm belief in the incarnation,[5] resurrection, and exaltation. The church's gospel story is retold because Christ's attitude of humbling Himself is the highest example of the mind-set needed by the Philippians to overcome their division.

"Your attitude should be the same as that of Christ Jesus," begins Paul's lesson. If there was ever an example of selflessness, it is that shown by Jesus. Visualize a giant "V" reaching from the highest part of the ceiling to the lowest part of the floor and then returning to the highest vantage point again. Listen to the song that illustrates the condescension and the climaxing exaltation:

> Who, being in very nature God,
>   did not consider equality with God
>   something to be grasped,
> but made himself nothing,
>   taking the very nature of a servant,
>   being made in human likeness (2:6-7).

This part of the old hymn reveals how different was Jesus the Second Adam from the First Adam we read about in Genesis (cp. I Corinthians 15:45). That Adam sought to become equal with God (Genesis

---

[5]Cp. John 1:1-14; Galatians 4:4-5; Colossians 1:15-19; Hebrews 1.

3:5). He was *self-seeking* while the Second Adam was *self-giving*. Jesus emptied Himself in the service of mankind (cp. Mark 10:45). Adam number one fell before the tempter (Genesis 3:5). Adam number two conquered the lure to be served rather than to serve. The Adam of the Genesis story coveted what he did not possess. The Adam of the gospel story was willing to lay aside His glory for you and me. Let us understand that while Jesus never emptied Himself of His deity, He gladly emptied Himself of His glory to bring redemption to men.[6] The song goes on:

> And being found in appearance as a man,
>   he humbled himself
>   and became obedient to death —
>   even death on a cross! (2:8).

Talk about an example of humility. Deity takes on humanity with its mortality, so He can die in our place. He lives not in a palace but takes "the very nature of a servant." Not ony does He die for sinners, He chooses to give His life through the torture of a crucifixion with all its accompanying scourging, mocking and jeering.

Should we choose to follow Jesus'example, all self-interest will be put aside for the sake of others. Our pride will have no last say. Our cross will be taken up gladly to reach the lost. Once *Christ-minded* (2:5), we will become *single-minded* (2:2).

Have you seen the popular bracelets some young people wear today with the letters on them of WWJD? When you ask their meaning, the response is that the

---

[6]John 17:1,5; 14:9.

letters represent the question "*What Would Jesus Do?*" This hymn of Chapter Two is the answer telling what Christ did. The last stanza goes on to tell what God the Father then did. It reads:

> Therefore God exalted him to the highest place
> and gave him the name that is above every name,
> that at the name of Jesus every knee should bow,
> in heaven and on earth and under the earth.
> and every tongue confess that Jesus Christ is Lord,
> to the glory of God the Father" (2:9-11).

After the supreme example of humility seen in Christ, the other examples seem small but well worthy of mention. Timothy "takes a genuine interest in your welfare," writes the Apostle, while another "looks out for his own interests" (2:20-21). He adds, "[Epaphroditus] almost died for the work of Christ, "risking his life" (2:30). The final human example of selflessness is Paul himself who was willing to be "poured out as a drink-offering" (2:17 footnote in ASV). He who could have been filled with pride at his tradition, birth, position, caste, religion, reputation, and character (items listed in 3:4-8) now labels them all "rubbish."

In the light of such self-less souls, the twin vices of "selfish ambition and vain conceit" (2:3) must be refused entrance at the door of every congregation. "Let your gentleness be evident to all" (4:5) is the proper sign to appear at the doorway of the church where a gentle spirit is what is needed to disarm any adversary. Divisions rise from *self-seeking*, but vanish with *self-renunciation*.

When the Lord's followers, starting with the Senior Citizens, demonstrate Christ's characteristics, healing of any rift is just around the corner. Putting other persons first with a willingness to look up to all and look down on none will solve most any trouble that could arise. Such *meekness* is not *weakness* but rather God-given strength for victory.

Our Lord Himself was "gentle and humble in heart" (Matthew 11:29), ever admonishing His disciples that "everyone who exalts himself will be humbled, and he who humbles himself will be exalted" (Luke 18:14). The only accusation that can be brought against the Christian faith is that some of its adherents have, on occasion, not been Christ-like enough. Paul's concern appears not to be that at the end of time the members of the church will be *raptured*. It is rather that in the present time the church's unity may be *ruptured*. Let us who wear the name of Christ not try to get *ahead of* each other. Let us rather agree to go forward *with* each other. The walls of modern day Jerichos will still fall down when we each blow the trumpet of the Lord. Should we each in pride blow our own horn, no enemy wall will even show a small hair-crack.

C. Senior Saints Never Finish Unifying the Workers by Being More Focused in Gospel

Some preachers should be arrested for mountain-climbing over mole-hills. They harangue over minor issues, dividing the congregation when they have been called to announce the major truths that are part and parcel of the gospel of Christ.

What the Sacred Scriptures in Philippians call upon us

to make known is the gospel. Nine times in the four chapters Paul uplifts the gospel. In the first chapter we read of "partnership in the gospel" (1:5), "confirming the gospel" (1:7), "advance the gospel" (1:12), "defense of the gospel" (1:16) and "worthy of the gospel" (1:27).

The Christian who longs for harmony among Jesus' disciples can see how worshipers join in songs that honor Christ and how they splinter into small groups through sermons that turn from central fundamentals of faith to peripheral opinions on issues that are not essential to salvation.[7] A sectarian gets worked up over what is not basic. Keep your teaching Christ-centered and you contribute to Christian oneness. In Philippians alone, in the 104 verses, the various names of Jesus appear 51 times. Who He was and what He did is worthy of proclamation.

Being theological bloodhounds is not our Christ-given commission. Teaching a self-help message is not preaching the gospel. Distributing religious aspirin to overcome lack of self esteem is not equal to sharing the good news of what Jesus did.

The minutia of human opinions (over the rapture, the best way to increase church attendance, what holidays a congregation ought to observe, or any other nonessential) is not to replace "the old, old story of Jesus and His love."

If someone wants to argue, yield like air in matters of human interest and feeling, but stand like valiant soldiers against the inroads of a substitute gospel.

---

[7]See Romans 14:1–15:13.

D. Senior Saints Never Finish Unifying the Workers by Being More Christ-like in Life

The existence of Christianity is dependent on the life Jesus lived. Its extension, however, depends to a great extent on the life we live. A critical question each of us needs to ask is, "Do I know I am saved?" and of equally vital importance is "Do the people around me know I'm saved?" Your *possession* of Christ will have more influence on your neighborts than your *profession* of Christ. What could defeat the church's proclamation will not be "higher criticism" of the Bible but lower living on the part of the believer. While we do wish for more Christian people, we also desire persons to be more Christian.

Each member of the church is a reflection *of* Christ or a reflection *on* Christ. So as Paul pleads for maintaining unity in 4:1-3, he also asks for each recipient of his letter to maintain virtue in 4:4-9. Whoever would have a neighbor or relative learn what Jesus can do for him or her, it is essential that you demonstrate what Christ has done for you. When a convert puts the Savior on the inside, he can demonstrate the truth of the gospel by letting Jesus show on the outside.

Let every reader translate into life the meaning of the character description Paul gives of what is "true . . . noble . . . right . . . pure . . . lovely . . . admirable . . . excellent . . . praiseworthy" (4:8). This octave of virtues lived becomes subjective aids to oneness and to evangelistic success.

Philippians: Love Letter

Since "our citizenship is in heaven" (3:20), it is to be expected that we would look different, talk different and act different from those amongst whom we dwell. With names inscribed in heaven, lives governed from heaven, and aspirations centered in heaven, it is natural that "your manner of life" (1:27, ASV) or your behavior among "a crooked and depraved generation" will be observable as "you shine like stars in the universe" (2:15). The *casual morals* of the present generation is certain to produce the *moral casualty* of our society. More than at any other time, the younger generation must see the Senior Saints modeling the new-life-style enabled by the grace of God.

You may not live in Salt Lake City, Utah, but Paul is right in calling you "saints in Christ Jesus" from the first verse to the end (1:1, cp. 4:21-22). You have been "filled with the fruit of righteousness that comes through Jesus Christ" (1:11). That is the only way it comes. Human attainment unaided can never reach such a height. Of the 51 times the word "saint" (ἅγιος) is in the Scriptures, Philippians 4:21 is the only time it is in the singular. This implies that each individual person in the Philippian congregation, as well as yours, is to grow in sainthood. Not one of them, or of us, is to feel excluded.

When the roll call of the redeemed is given, asking each of us if we have labored for Christian oneness, I hope all of us will respond "present" to inquiry as to prayer, humility, gospel priority and Christian character.

Conclusion

ooks have conclusions. Operas and dramas write *finis* at the end. A life lived for Christ has no ending. We in our senior years as Christians know that "in Christ" we will live forever. What we do not yet know is how much longer that God-given life will be spent on earth before it will be continued in heaven.

It is our prayer that, having listened to Paul's words to the Philippians, our final years here will be the most meaningful of all. Believing in the inspiration of the Scriptures, we recognize that the epistle of our study is more than a letter from Paul to a church in his day. It is a letter from God to us in our time. If you would have the "mind of Christ" (2:5, ASV), the joy of Christ (3:1), the righteousness of Christ (3:9), and the strength of Christ (4:13), remember where all these blessings are to be found — "in Christ" (1:1). Only a Stoic aims at total independence from everyone. The Christian knows his life is completely dependent upon Christ.

May I encourage you to answer your mail. If someone has cared enough to correspond with me, I sense a responsibility to reply. God's concern for the salvation and happiness of each of us, so evident in this love letter of Philippians, is waiting for a live response. The Savior would love to hear from you. He hopes for you to respond today.

"The grace of the Lord Jesus Christ be with your spirit. Amen" (4:23).[1]

---

[1]This is a common benediction used by Paul here and in Galatians 6:18 and Philemon 25.